SPIRITUAL
GIFT

BOOK OF POETRY

Written by
CHRIS GORDON

Inspired by The Holy Spirit

ISBN 978-1-64458-435-4 (paperback)
ISBN 978-1-64458-436-1 (digital)

Christian Faith Publishing, Inc.
832 Park Avenue
Meadville, PA 16335
www.christianfaithpublishing.com

Printed in the United States of America

I would like to first give thanks to the Almighty God, the creator of all thing. To my Lord and Savior Jesus Christ. I confess with my mouth that you are Lord, and I believe in my heart that God raised you from the dead. Lord I thank you for this gift that you have given me, and now I dedicate back to you what you have given me first. To my beautiful wife Cabrina Gordon. You're the reason I returned from the path I was on, back to my first love. Thank you for being so patient, so kind; so understanding and so persistence. I love you and I always will. To my church family at Destiny Christian Ministry. To Prophetess Moore. Thanks for everything. For believing in me, when I was secretly doubting myself. Thank you for your words of encouragement, your words of advice, and most of all, your teaching the truth. You are truly a woman of God. To my parents Mr. & Mrs. Isaac and Barbara Gordon. Even though the two of you are not here to see this in the physical, I know you're watching in the spiritual. To my sisters. Christine Gordon (my twin), Leadrienne Gordon, and Deadrienne Gordon (her twin). Thanks girls, for never giving up on me or turning your backs to me, even when the world did. To Adrian A. Gordon Sr, my brother. You do the dirt and I get the blame (lol). To my nephews, and nieces, Kailan Johnson, Tyrence Williams, Adrian A. Gordon Jr., Charity Bethancourt, De'Asianay Gordon, De'Arielle Zenon, Ta'Shalynn Davis, LeAryalynn Bourgeios, Akaijah Travis, Amiya Gordon, and Dalaisha Zenon. I'm proud of and love each and every one of you dearly. Keep up the good work. To Malasia Bradford, I'm proud of how far you've come, the process you've made, and the lesson you've learned. You'll forever have a place in my heart. To my daughter Destiny B Gordon and my grandson Matthew Gordon. May God forever keep his mighty hands of protection around you both and may his love and grace forever cover the both of you. To the newest addition in our lives, Genesis S Gordon. Your presence has made our lives more exciting and enjoyable. We thank God for blessing us with you. In our hearts and our lives are the two places you'll forever remain. In our world is where you'll forever be. And all of our love, you'll forever have. To my two best friends, Christopher Sanders and Anthony Griffin. You guys are the true meaning of friendship. To Christian Faith Publishing. To those of you I haven't mention, it's because time and space won't allow me. And just because you're not on paper, doesn't mean you're not in my heart. God bless you all.

Praise and Worship

Praise the Lord! Praise God in His sanctuary; praise Him in His mighty heaven!

Praise Him for His mighty works; praise His unequaled greatness!

Praise Him with a blast of the rams' horn; praise Him with the lyre and harp!

Praise Him with the tambourine and dancing; praise Him with strings and flutes!

Praise Him with a clash of cymbals; praise Him with loud clanging cymbals!

Let everything with breath sing praises to the Lord! (Psalms 150:1–6 New Living Translation)

Contents

God's Word

Your words I've hidden in my heart
That I might not sin against you
I've likened them to plumb bobs from my heart
Weights that hold builders plumb line straight and true

I measure my own thoughts, feelings, and behavior
By your word, not the other way around
So no matter what the circumstances are, I'll know
My house is built on solid ground

When you find time on your hands
Put them together in prayer
Give thanks to the Lord God above
For His word assures us He's always there

We can take His presence with us
All through the day
We can talk to him frequently
By blending His word with prayers, work, and play

God Is Good

The Lord is my shepherd
I shall not want
He has mercy on my soul
I cannot front

In the presence of my enemy
He prepares a table for me
And when I look toward heaven
His handiwork I see

He restores my soul
In green pastures I eat
I walk not with the ungodly
Because He guides my feet

Beside the still waters
He allows me to stand
And when I'm wandering in the wilderness
He holds my hand

Raindrop

Have you ever heard a raindrop
As it falls to the ground?
Have you ever heard it tapping on the rooftops?
How relaxing is the sound

Have you ever played outside
While the rain falls on you?
You make believe the clouds were crying
Pretend they were hurting too

Have you ever used the raindrops
As a tool to hide your tears?
And each time you wipe your face
You wipe away your fears

Have you ever watched the raindrop
To the point where you almost cried
And you thought it was a message from God
Saying He knows how you feel inside

What He's Done for Me

God is good
God is great
The sinner He loves
The sin He hates

He gave His only begotten Son
Who died upon the cross
So that even though we're lost in sin
Our souls will not be lost

He lifts us up with a mighty hand
And with mercy and grace
He plants our feet on solid ground
So one day we'll see His face

He gives us living water
So we will never thirst
And he who finish last in life
In heaven he is first

In this fleshly world I may be nothing
But to Him I'm the most
So He gave me three important things in life
His self, His Son, His Holy Ghost

All These Years

Couldn't see the forest for the trees
Or heaven for the stars
Couldn't appreciate being free
Until locked behind bars

Never really miss the water
Until the well ran dry
Never knew how strong I was
Until it was time to cry

Never knew who lifted me up
Until I actually fell down
Never knew how far I'd come
Until I turned around

Never knew how fast I was moving
Until I started to take things slow
Never knew what I was missing
Until it was time to let it go

Never knew who was carrying me
Until times got hard
Never knew who I could call on
Until it was time to call on God

Surrender

Intimacy with God should be your greatest goal
Fix your eyes firmly on the things above
Don't let anything come between you and Him
Lord, I want you above all others, abide within His love

Don't bow to the world's low moral standards
Or dilute the truth for the sake of some
Let your marriage to Christ be unbreakable
Be all that God would have it to become

Whenever you need reassurance
As to your place in God's eye
Study the scriptures, show yourself approved
Don't let your days pass you by

By the time you're halfway through
You'll know to whom you belong
Give yourself totally to Him
Praise Him through words and song

Let loose and quit worrying what others think
Is a good way to start
The only thing you need to care about
Is Jesus loves you and you love Him with all your heart

Question

When the present is daunting
And the past is haunting
Where do you turn for release?

When you can't hide your pride
Or what's inside
To whom do you go for comfort and peace?

What a Friend

He was rich in His person
For He is Eternal God
He was rich in His possession
For He is King of Kings, Lord of Lords

He was rich in His powers
Therefore, sin He abhors
He was rich in heaven and earth
But gave it up to become poor

He united Himself to mankind
And took on human skin
He gave up His riches in heaven
Traded it for my earthly sin

He was laughed at, He was mocked
They even spat in His face
So that I could become heir of the Kingdom with Him
He endured that kind of disgrace

He left the throne to become a servant
All that He had was lost
With nowhere on earth to lie His head
He took on my sins and died upon the cross

Thank You

Thank you for making me just like you
Thank you for doing the things you do
Thank you for coming from above
Thank you for teaching me how to love

Thank you for guiding my feet
Thank you for the food I eat
Thank you for the toils and snare
Thank you for the clothes I wear

Thank you for having mercy on my soul
Thank you for cleansing me making me whole
Thank you for teaching me how to pray
Thank you for blessing me to see another day

Thank you for stress and strife
Thank you for the breath of life
Thank you for courage, thank you for hope
Thank you for comfort at the end of my rope

Thank you for being a friend
Thank you for bearing my sin
Thank you for loving me most
Thank you for the Holy Ghost

Thank you for joy, thank you for pain
Thank you for sunshine, thank you for rain
Thank you for night, thank you for day
I even thank you for these words I say

Thank you for ups, thank you for downs
Thank you for planting my feet on solid ground
Thank you for heaven, thank you for earth
Thank you for death, thank you for birth

Thank you for forgiveness, thank you for strength
Thank you for second chances, so I could repent
Thank you for this song my heart now sings
Lord, I thank you for everything

When I Need Him Most

From day to day I struggle with sin
Not knowing if tomorrow will ever come
For forgiveness and love I pray to God
Where all my strength comes from

He's my comforter, healer, Savior, and friend
In my darkest hour, he's my guiding light
He hears my cry, answers my prayers
On Him I meditate day and night

He lifts me up when I'm down
Makes me feel rich when I don't have a dime
He's my shelter in the midst of the storm
He's my strength in trouble times

He gives me what I ask of Him
The door is open when I knock
When the rain descends, and the flood comes
My house still stands, for it is founded on a solid rock

Imagine This

Jesus has done something for me
That no one else would
He gave up everything He had in heaven
To die on earth so I could live good

I could picture Him in heaven
Talking to His dad like this
Saying, "Heavenly Father, you know what
Let me go down to earth to die for old Chris"

"I'll get me twelve disciples
The thirteen of us will make everyone we can believe
I'll feed, I'll heal, I'll teach, I'll preach
Then I'll pass it on to them before I leave"

"So by the time old Chris becomes
Isaac and Barbra Gordon's son
He'll sin for a while but in the end
He'll do what needs to be done"

"I've got a feeling he won't be ashamed
Not even of the things he used to do
He'll be one of the reasons I'm lifted up
Letting others know I died for their sins too"

"And because I gave up my life for his
He's gonna let the whole world know
That he used to do the same thing they're doing
He's been there, done that, don't need it no mo'"

"And by the time he gets married
Have respectable kids and a submissive wife
He'll thank me every day for dying for his sins
'Cause now he knows how it feels to live the good life."

Thank You, Lord

Heavenly Father, I thank you
For having mercy on my soul
Thank you for sparing my life in spite of my sins
And not destroying me like in the days of old

Thank you for giving me a second chance
For true love like a bridegroom to his wife
Thank you for giving me your only begotten son
So that I may have eternal life

Thank you for showing me
What patient and true love could do
So when I look back at those troubled times in life
I'll know who those one set of footprints belong to

Thank you for blessing me to see
Walk, talk, and hear
Thank you for warning me
That the kingdom of heaven is near

Thank you, Heavenly Father,
For chastising me
For if it had not been for you
O where would I be

I'm Encouraged

When my smile is a frown
'Cause I'm feeling down
And my cheerful day becomes blue

With nowhere to go
'Cause I'm feeling low
Lord, I turn to you

You pick me up
Fill my cup
Turn me completely around

Those cheerful days that turn blue
Now the sun shines through
My frowns are now turned upside down

I'm Your Servant

I'm your servant Lord
I'm here for you to use
Let your will be done
I'll do whatever you choose

If you want me to do it
With your blessing it'll be done
And even though the battle is not over
I know that the victory is won

I'll be that city on a hill
So the whole world could see
That lamp that sits on a stand
Let your light shine through me

I'll share my wealth with the poor
The hungry I'll feed
I'll live my life like your word says
A living bible for those who cannot read

The Name of Jesus

One day as I was walking
I thought it was the Lord's name I heard
When I turned to see who was talking
All I saw was a little bird

So I kept going about my way
And I thought I heard it again
When I turned to see who it was this time
It was only the whistling of the wind

Then I heard it a third time
I thought, *Now who could this be?*
Even though I hesitated, I still turned
Only to see the waving of leaves in a tree

So I started to think, *Am I hearing things?*
Is my mind playing some sort of game?
That was when the Spirit revealed to me that God was so special
Even nature whispered His name

I Am (1)

I am the way, the truth, and the life
No man cometh unto the Father but by me
I am bread for the hungry, water for the thirsty,
Eyes so the blind could see

I am love to the brokenhearted
Comfort for the uneasy soul
When drowning in the sea of life
I am the hand to grab hold

I Am (2)

Strong enough to move mountains
Weak enough to shed tears
Man enough to walk away
Faithful enough to overcome fears

Clever enough to know where I'm going
Conscious enough to gather my thoughts
Willing enough to share the moment
Loving enough to open my heart

Brave enough to knock until the door is opened
Curious enough to seek until I find
Confident enough to express how I feel
Bold enough to speak my mind

Happiness

You smile for no reason
And everyone knows
That it's the Spirit of God within
On your face it shows

All blessings are bestowed upon you
On the mysteries of His secrets you wait
You know, that you know, that you know
Your strength lies in your faith

There's a bounce in your step
In your ear there's a ring
From your heart you sing the song in your head
You thank Him for everything

There's a feeling of peace
That you feel inside
You can humble yourself
And release your pride

Happiness is being content
Knowing God is not far
No matter your circumstances or situation
You know He's wherever you are

What If

What if you had powers
To tell mountains to get out of your way
And just by the sound of your voice
They would obey

What if you had the ability
To make everything bow to your command
Without even touching, move things
Just by the wave of your hand

What if you could speak things into existence
Live your life how you want it to be
Make the wind obey you
And your voice calm the sea

What if I told you these are the things
You could already do
All you need is faith the size of a grain of a mustard seed
And belief in the God that lives in you

Never Satisfied

The children of Israel were a lot like Pharaoh
They saw God's miraculous signs
But still they hardened their hearts
And constantly changed their minds

He gave them bread from heaven
When they complained there was nothing to eat
They ate 'til they were full
Then cried there was no meat

So He opened up the windows of heaven again
Fed them meat for a whole month
Yet they still complained
The more He gave the more they wanted

God told Moses, "These are a stiff necked people
They're never satisfied, they complain and fuss."
Aren't yesterday's Israelites
A lot like us?

God picked them up then
Like He does us today
And as soon as we can't get what we want
What's the first thing we say

"I was better off where I was,
Please Lord cut me some slack."
Like Lots wife when God destroyed Sodom and Gomorrah
We can't move forward 'cause we keep looking back

We can always remember how it used to be
Things were good because of a little money
We want something new without giving up the old
Refusing to enter the land of milk and honey

Super Bowl Sunday

Today is the Lord's day
But it's also Super Bowl Sunday
The Lord won't mind I thought to myself;
If I miss church just this one day

I turned the TV on, started channel surfing
To see what time the game was to be played
With the remote in my hand, game on my mind
On the couch is where I lay

I got everything I need for the game
Today is gonna be a blast
Kick off is at one o'clock p.m. 'til then
ESPN highlights of Super Bowls past

Then I saw a Jesus saves commercial
As I strolled past channel three
It said, "If Christ was to come back right now,
Where would you be?"

That question stuck in my head
I thought to myself, *You fool*
Then I found myself getting dressed
Saying, "If He comes back right now, I'll be in Sunday school."

God's Turn

When your situation is absolutely impossible
And you feel from trouble you can't hide
That's God favorite time to work in your life
When you feel absolutely disqualified

That's when God says, "Get out of the way
Watch and learn
For you tried to overcome this yourself
Now it's my turn."

What Can I Say

For the Lord God has brought me
Along life's narrow way
Because of His mercy and grace, He's delivered me
Up until this very day

He's been better to me than I've been to myself
He's been more than just a friend
He's comforted me in my times of sorrow
He's been there through thick and thin

When I had nowhere else to turn
Nowhere else to go
He was the shelter that protected me
He's done all great things just to let me know

According to His words
There's no other God but Him
He keeps His promise, His words are true
Forever blessed I'll be

A Perfect Father

One of God's purpose in pain
Is to brand the image of Jesus in our heart
So that whatever the world places before us
From that image we'll never depart

Keep your eyes on Jesus
You'll lose sight of your fears
Trust in the Lord and He'll wipe
Your cheek stained with tears

Our only hope here below
Is help from God above
His grace, His mercy, His forgiveness
His dying to protect His love

Discovering

Imagine receiving a gift without wrapping paper
The joy would be short-lived
For much of the excitement is in the anticipation
Of finding out what gifts are given

Apparently God created us with a normal setting
That causes us to enjoy the process of discovery
Because finding something is more exciting
Than having it in plain view to see

He could have revealed all truth to all people
At the very beginning of time
But He chose to reveal Himself gradually
So that those who diligently seek could find

He's not playing a cruel game of hide and seek
The truth is right there hovering
About who He is and what He's doing
But He allows us to enjoy the process of discovering

God Loves Us

The weak, the helpless, and the discouraged
Are in the shepherd's care
He gives us our breath, clothing, food, and shelter
For the things we have need of He's aware

He provides those needs in our relationship with Him
He speaks to us through His word
He wants us to pour out our hearts to Him about everything
Even our longing to be loved and heard

We can find Him to be our rock and refuge
In Him we can place our trust
For He gave His only begotten son
To prove His love for us

There will be no death, nor sorrow, nor crying
There will be no more pain
He will one day bring an end to the unnatural rule of Satan
And begin His righteous reign

God's Goodness

Sometimes I wonder
Where would I be
If God hadn't intervened in my life
And saved me

True indeed I've been in
Some messed-up places
I'm able to remember situations
But can't remember faces

Staring eye to eye with a pistol
Thinking now what will I do
Wondering if I'll still be alive tomorrow
To tell what I've just been through

I now know one thing
When all is said and done
That the only reason I'm still alive today
Is to testify to everyone

That God so loved the world
That He gave His only begotten son
So that we're saved not by what we do
But by trusting what He has done

Witness

Before Jesus ascended to His father
He gave His disciples a final command
To be His witness throughout the world
To launch a worldwide witness campaign

The Holy Ghost would give them supernatural powers
To be bold, faithful, credible witnesses to spread His word
They were to go into the world where people didn't know Him
And give truthful account of what they
had seen, experienced, and heard

Like the disciples God left us to witness to the world
Being a witness means telling the truth
to others about what we know
We're to take the gospel to the end of the earth
Meaning telling the truth about Jesus where'er we go

Point-Blank

The things you want your flesh to do
That's what the flesh will do
You should have control over the flesh
The flesh shouldn't have control over you

If we lust after a woman or material things
And have no kind of shame
It's because we choose to do those things
No one else is to blame

We use the excuse the mind is willing
But the flesh is weak
We use the scripture as a cover
For the thing we ourselves seek

Money, sex, drugs, and alcohol
Are the things we use to have fun
When the money, drugs, and alcohol lead to
something incurable from the sex
Then we beg God to forgive us for what we've done

We let our flesh controls our minds
We know one of the seven deadly sins is greed
But instead of saying, "Lord help me with this problem,"
We say, "These are the things I need."

We know we should love our neighbors
Since the beginning of time that's the way God meant it to be
Turn the other cheek for us means turn our back on our brother
If I help him, what's in it for me

It's a cold world and people don't care about others
It's sad but it's true
A perfect example, what the apostle Paul meant
By the things I will to do, I do not do

Ye cannot drink the cup of the Lord and the cup of the devil
Ye cannot be partakers of the two
Ye will either have control over the flesh by doing the will of God
Or ye will serve the devil by letting the flesh control you

Common Cents

Mark chapter twelve we read of a widow's sacrifice
She gave a fraction of a penny, which was all of her living
This widow's sacrifice was an example and encouragement
The priceless gift of giving

This poor woman had put in more than everyone else
Jesus said therefore she shall be uplifted
For God looks at the heart not the hand
The giver not the gift

Recovery

It takes faith to get through life's struggles
Even when times are hard
It takes faith to be a good father
A good husband and a man of God

I'm a recovering addict who's been privileged to fall in love
With a god who never saw me as broken and bruised
He took fragments of my broken heart, sealed them with His grace
His one sheep out of a hundred He refused to lose

He favorably polished my new heart like a rare diamond
I'm a precious jewel in His sight
And the greatest miracle is that I now believe what he says
That I'm salt of the earth a candlestick that gives light

Times like These

Every time I take one step forward
I get pushed back two
I can never seem to get it right
No matter what I try to do

Seems like bad luck hangs over me
Like a black cloud above my head
One minute I'm happy to be here
Next minute I'm wishing I was dead

Sometimes I just want to give up
'Cause I feel like I can't win
Every time something good happens
Bad creeps right back in

Then I called on God one day,
"Lord, help me I'm stuck
Have mercy on me, Heavenly Father,
Can't anybody have this much bad luck?"

Then I heard His voice say to me.
"I've always been with you, my child
To understand the good, you had to endure the bad
So I allowed you to suffer a while."

Although I never appreciated how good He's been
I now look forward to Him pulling me through
I'm finally ready to give Him thanks and praise
God knows it's long overdue

Somebody Was Praying for Me

No matter how I look at it
It's all perfectly clear
That with all the foolishness I've done
I'm blessed to still be here

From kicking in dope dealers' doors
Robbing them just to have fun
Thinking that I was invincible
While looking down the barrel of a gun

To drinking until I couldn't remember a thing
Then jumping behind the wheel to drive
Flipping the car two or three times
Saying I was unstoppable 'cause I was still alive

I've had unprotected sex
With just about every female I've ever met
While a friend of mine had unprotected sex once
And full-blown AIDS was the cause of his death

I've smoked marijuana, I've done cocaine
Then laughed at the next man 'cause he was hooked on crack
Failure to realize that it was the mercy and grace of God
That kept me from going too far down that
same road to not be able to come back

I've been to jail numerous of times
Unable to see it was God's way of giving me a second chance
And every time He would grant me back my freedom
I was back to the same old song just a different dance

Finally, I decide to surrender my life to Him
So as I look back, now it's perfectly clear to see
That the reason I escaped death and still here to talk about it
Is because somebody was praying for me

Sometimes I Wonder

Is there really a place called heaven?
Or someplace below called hell
And if so what are they really like
No one who's been there has been able to come back and tell

It's been said, "In this place called heaven
The streets are paved with gold
There's no more sickness, no more sorrow
No pain, no strife is what I'm told"

And this place called hell they say
It's the worst-case scenario you can think
You'll spend eternity in pain and suffering
A lake of fire with no water to drink

Some have even gone as far as to say
That heaven and hell is right here on earth
It's being at peace or at war
It's your state of mind from birth

Is there really a place called heaven and hell?
And do souls really go there when the body dies?
God's word says there is such a place
And God's word tells no lies

Then God Stepped In

Before I found Jesus
My life was a mess
There wasn't anything I wouldn't do
I could care less

About you, you, you, even myself
At times it would seem
I'd kick in a man's door
And take everything from drugs to dreams

We could do this the easy way or the hard
Pay attention to what I'm saying
Then I'd put my pistol to his head
To let him know I ain't playing

Get in, get out as quick as possible
Was always the plan
Leaving the victim tied up on the floor
Wondering who was that masked man

Then one night the game
Took a drastic turn
An ugly situation
A lesson well learned

The game of hunter catch rabbit
Was no longer fun
A perfect night for hunting
But this time the rabbit had the gun

Like every other night on every other hunt
My heart was boldly drumming
Only this time when I kicked in the door
It was like the rabbit knew I was coming

I looked in his eyes, saw his grim-reaper smile
My brain quickly registered I'm through
I heard a loud bang, saw a blue flash of light
Right after he said, "I've been waiting on you"

He let off eight quick rounds and all I could do
I mumbled, "Lord, help me this is it"
And either his shot was off or God answered my prayer
'Cause out of eight rounds none of them hit

When the fire went out and the smoke finally cleared
I told myself with an ear-to-ear grin
I almost lost that round, then a voice whispered and said,
"You would have, if I hadn't stepped in"

God Said

The world that we now we live in
It's slowly coming to an end
A man's worst enemy
Is sometimes his own best friend

From the unemployment line to the president
Everyone's complaining times are hard
We're placing all our focus on rising prices
And none of it on God

We have to pull together as a nation
Yes, we can is planted in our head
We're putting all our trust in man
And forgetting what God has said

God said, "If you put your trust in Him
Everything will be okay
And not to worry about tomorrow
Sufficient for today"

If you seek His kingdom and His righteousness
All things will be added unto you
He said, "I know the things you have need of
So don't worry like the Gentiles do"

"If I so clothed the grass of the field
Will I not much more clothe you"
He said, "Lay up for yourselves treasures in heaven
For where your treasure is there your heart will be too"

You Never Know

If the master of the house had known what hour
That the thief would be coming through
Wouldn't He have watched and not allowed
His house to be broken into

If the five foolish virgins had taken their lamps
And brought some oil along with them
Wouldn't they've been ready when the bridegroom came
And not shut out from the wedding without Him

If the evil servant left in charge
Knew when his master would return would you think
That he would have beaten his fellow servants
And with the drunkard beginning to eat and drink

Therefore, I say, watch for the coming of the Lord
For you know neither the day nor the hour
Be sober, be vigilant, because your adversary the devil
Walks about like a roaring lion seeking whom he may devour

Eat the Word

My stomach is big
That means I could hold a lot
My mouth is wide
So I could eat all you got

My food is God's word
And I eat it every day
I'm always greedy with it
But greed in a good way

Meaning the more I eat the more I want
It's food for my soul
I get it hot out the oven (the Bible)
Because I don't like my food cold

My appetizer is Matthew chapters five through seven
My main course is Colossian chapter three
My wine is Ephesians five and eighteen, it lets me know
After a meal like this, filled with the Spirit I'll be

Lack of Appreciation

I never took the time to sit and watch
How an ant could climb a wall
And wonder how it could do that
Accomplish that incredible feat and not fall

I never just sit back and wonder
How birds know exactly when to fly south
I never paid attention to two bugs fighting
And wondered what they were disputing about

I never took the time out
To think about the unusual things
Like is that noise that dolphins make words or laughter
Or what is that song the humming bird sings

I never knew if you touch a moth's wings
It'll no longer be able to fly
I never really thought about what was meant by the old saying,
"You never miss your water until the well runs dry"

Not just me, sometimes other people of faith
Never stop to show appreciation
Born believers in Christ
Who never thank God for His creation

I never took the time to thank God
For the breath of life, the greatest gift ever
I never slowed down to even think about stopping
It was always never, never, never

It took my going to jail to slow down
And listen to what God had to say
I never thought concrete walls and razor wires
Would teach me to appreciate God waking me up every day

Heavenly Father, Earthly Dad

My heavenly father and earthly dad
Are two of the same
They both provide my every need
Whenever I call their name

The two of them let me know
They do for me because I'm their child
As long as I'm obedient to their will
They'll do the things that make me smile

My heavenly father says, "He will never forsake me
Nor will He leave me alone"
My earthly dad, whenever I ask of him
Gives me bread and not stone

I love the two of them dearly
Both their words are true
My heavenly father, my earthly dad
I could never decide who's the greater of the two

Until one night I past his bedroom
And I heard my earthly dad
Talking to my heavenly father
Thanking Him for all we had

That's when I knew who was the greatest
I realized then all the things I had
Was provided by my heavenly father
Given to me through my earthly dad

Tell Me How

How can you hide something from someone
Who already knows everything
What kind of gift do you give someone
Who already knows what you'll bring

How do you get away from someone
That you can't outrun
How can you conceal something from someone
Who already knows in your heart, what you've done

How can you be impatient with someone
Who'll do anything for you, if you've got faith
How can you be angry with someone
Who knows no hate

How can you befriend someone
Who's done nothing for you but lied
And not love the only person
Who for you, gave His life and died

Clipped Wing Fix

A little bird flew from a tree to my backyard
As I stood on my porch one day
While it looked around for whatever it was looking for
A cat was slowly creeping its way

I thought to myself, *National Geographic*
Live and up close
Will the little bird make it away safe
Will the little bird get toasted

The cat got closer and closer
It was like the little bird couldn't see
At the last minute he tried to fly away
Cat clipped his wing, if only he'd stayed in that tree

Having compassion, I scared the cat off
Before he made the little bird his meal of the day
I got the little bird's clipped wing fix
And watched over him 'til he was able to fly away

In real life, we're that little bird, the backyard is the world
Where we get caught in the mix
Satan is the cat that clips our wings, our heart
Jesus is the one looking from the porch of
heaven, who gets our clipped wing fixed

Action Speaks Louder than Words

You say you love the Lord
Because He gave His life for you
You can quote every scripture in the Bible
Yet refuse to do what God asks you to

Don't judge others
Yet you still point the finger
Don't worry about tomorrow
Yet doubt still lingers

You go to church every Sunday
And hear the preacher preach the word
Yet from Monday to Saturday
It's like you forgot what you've heard

Revenge is mine sayeth the Lord
But you refuse to turn the other cheek
Love your neighbor like you love yourself
To you is a sign of being weak

You never control your tongue
You talk how words can kill
You say you love the Lord
Yet you refuse to do His will

You, O Lord

You remember me in my weakness
You saved me from my enemy
You give food to every living thing
You made the heavens so skillfully

You placed the earth among the waters
You made the heavenly light
The sun to rule by day
The moon and stars to rule by night

You taught me to pray for the needs of others
Because you already know what's in my heart
You already know my wants and desires
You created me, you know my every thought

Therefore, I put my trust in you
To help me overcome my selfish greed
You said if I obey your commands and decrees
You'll supply my every need

You're my shepherd, if I ask of you anything
Having faith, it will be done
You showed me how much you loved me
By giving your only son

Don't Get Caught Up

Lord, make me to know my end
What is the measure of my days
That I may know how frail I am
Guide me, show me thine ways

And now, Lord, what do I wait for
All my hope is in you
Deliver me from all my transgressions
Watch over all I do

Who will not fear you, O King of the Nations
For this is your rightful due
For among all the wise men of the Nations
And in all their kingdoms, there's none like you

Of course, I will never be your equal
Yet you desire to call me friend
And the reason I can look forward to eternity
Is because you've wiped out the effects of sin

Think about What You're Thinking About

Our biggest problem is our way of thinking
Like Adam and Eve, we believe Satan's lies
And when we do, our loyalty to God
Is compromised

Then he slithers off to his next assignment
Leaving us alone to face our regrets
And the realization that his lies have seduced our thoughts
Leads us to fret

We should submit our thoughts to God
Because as a man thinketh so is he
The scripture says, "If you submit to God
And resist the devil, he'll flee"

Your thoughts control your words
Your words control what you do
What you do tells others about the person
That lives inside of you

Before anything becomes action
It is first conceived as a thought
Christ says, "This is what defiles the body
Because what you speak comes from your heart"

Evil thoughts produce evil actions
A bad tree cannot produce good fruits
Nourishment of the branches comes from the tree
Nourishment of the tree comes from the roots

Fix your thoughts on what is honorable
And right and pure and true
And lovely and admirable and those thoughts
Will display actions of the Christ in you

Consequences

We often live with the pain of consequences
From accepting bad advice or from the choices we make
But consequences are reminders of hard lessons
Not excuses to give up or to keep making the same mistakes

Worrying

The rich worry
About losing everything they got
The poor worry
About not having a lot

Worrying is sinful and produces fear
A disease causing other ills
It hinders you from receiving blessings
Blocking your faith in God's will

The righteous worry
About whether they'll go to hell
The wicked worry
About who'll find out the lies they tell

Worrying breaks down the immune system
Causes high blood pressure because of stress
It's the reason you toss and turn in bed at night
Unable to get a good night of rest

Once upon a Time

I was one of the devil's best soldiers
He hates that I got away
Every day he comes with his best temptation
Hoping he'll get me to stray

He's knows my strengths and my weakness
To tempt me, he knows how
To get me back I know he'll never stop trying
He's mad 'cause I'm God's soldier now

Joy Comes

There's no problem
Big or small
That God can't handle
Submit to Him your all

Cast on Him all your worries
Don't be ashamed
Give it all to Him in prayer
Believing in Jesus's name

Don't let what people do bother you
Don't let what they say steal your joy
The Bible says, "The devil comes to rob and steal
To kill and destroy."

So consider it a blessing when you endure pain
Count it as joy when you overcome sorrow
God allows pain and sorrow today
To open your heart to the joys of tomorrow

Don't Want To

I don't want to die like some of my friends
Not knowing what God has done for me
I don't want to continue being a slave to sin
Knowing God paid the ransom to set me free

I don't want to know what it feels like
To weather a storm or face my fear
Pour out my heart or call on Him
Then find out He's not here

I don't want to go through this life
Singing the same old song
About what I shoulda, coulda, or wouda done
Every time something goes wrong

I don't want to live seventy or eighty years
Just to have the things I say and do
Be the reason God says on judgment day,
"Get away from me, I don't know you"

I don't want to know what if feels like
Not to be able to call on Him
Or to live a life I think is righteous
And in the end be condemned

Nobody but God

As I look back on the beach of life
I can see God's footprints in the sand
And when I needed a pat on the back
I could feel His mighty hand

When I think about how long I've been running
I could feel Him wipe the sweat from my face
And when I was tired and felt like giving up
I could hear Him whisper, "Keep up the pace."

When my heart ached because of hardship
He gave me peace of mind
When I thought that I had nothing, He strengthened me
To patiently endure calamities of every kind

When I thought that He was wrong
For chastising me for something I'd done
I could hear Him say, "I do this
because I love you, my son.

The Earth Is the Lord's

Pay attention to the things around you
And you'll be able to see God's mighty hand
That the things designed were by a brilliant designer
And not the works of man

Let no one fool you into believing
That this world was created by some big bang
That that's the reason seasons come and go
And in the middle of nothing the world just hang

If that isn't bogus enough
There's another story scientists tell
That every living organism today
Originated from a single cell

First the big bang theory
Then the single-cell story
Why is it so hard to believe?
Why can't we just give God the glory

Is it because we can't see Him
The reason we don't give Him praise
Pay attention and you'll see Him through His creation
Look at how nights never get crossed with days

Look at how He created man in His image and likeness
How He made everything beautiful in its time
How the moon never comes out
When it's the sun's turn to shine

From the floor of the ocean
To the heavens above
No one can deny that the Earth is the Lord's
And the fullness thereof

Come in…a Look at the Heart

Man looks at the outside
God looks at the heart
He says, "To have a good relationship,
This is where we should start."

The heart, not the organ that pumps blood
But the inner being of the soul
The part deep down inside where secrets are kept
Where truth and lies are told

God said, "I stand at the door and knock,
If you hear my voice and open, I will come in."
He's saying, if you are willing to let Him into your heart
You can share a meal with Him as a friend

CPSIA information can be obtained
at www.ICGtesting.com
Printed in the USA
LVHW051557050121
675506LV00017B/958